I0777153

Introduction

How can you „read a person? How can you appoint faultlessly a person without getting a ten-year degree in psychology? Of course, you are not going to be as well as a psychologist, but the general characteristics of people are helpful in making you more aware of what someone's personality is like.

Analyzing people gives us a decisive superiority in business, social and personal cases. In spite the fact, the majority of individuals review each other instinctively, there are not many of us who manage all the time of this aptitude and grade it up, doing so provides interests that others don't pay attention to. This manual will teach you how to manage this. There are various characters of personalities. Everybody is specific, but still, you can find a lot about somebody just from monitoring what type of personality an individual fits into. There are universally adopted "types" that an individual could be, and once you look through and learn how to find it out, you can apply this information in a life. How can you use knowledge according to analyzing people if you don't know how to use this knowledge? This book will tell you how to read body language and personality cues it will give you actionable steps for using it. You can change your own state of mind by changing your body language.

How can the non-verbal and verbal clues help us to understand people better, sometimes even without words? How can you decode a personality after the first minutes of talking to him or her and after paying attention what gestures they use? People often represent themselves falsely to hide important information, get a hold of it from you or aimed at profit. This book will be your best booster in decoding them.

Table of Contents

Chapter One: The ultimate non-verbal clue cheat sheet

Beware of persons whose bellies do not move when they laugh

Chinese proverb

The interpersonal impact during people's communication depends frequently not only on our words, person's nonverbal messages may reduce or add the meaning to the words and expressions. The nonverbal cues announce people's expectations, their state of mind, self-awareness, giving an incentive to our entire that begins chattering continuously, exposing what we feel and think in fact.

Nonverbal communication is commonly evinced through non-linguistic means; it is such a distinctive feature of the humans, including the piece of factors affecting and stimulating the meaning of some events, such as smell and sound, space and time. Nonverbal communication includes vocal clues (volume of our voice, rate, pitch, voice tone with distinctive features); visual clues (eye movements, facial expressions, people's gestures, body orientation); signs and signals sent to the persons via color (a thing we usually don't pay attention to); proxemics clues (distance between conversation partners and space); clues provided via appearance (how a person looks like); smell clues (olfactory); time or chronemic clues. Nonverbal messages are usually sent by the individuals accidentally or consciously, their sense depends mostly on how they are interpreted. Nonverbal messages fulfill a metacommunicative function, explaining both the nature of our attitudes and the meaning of the verbal messages sent to both directions during a conversation. Based on the interpretations of the nonverbal cues, one may realize better if our partners like or dislike us from the first moments of conversation, accept and embrace our ideas and attitudes, interpret them, whether they want to encourage our relationship and continue the conversation, or terminate it right now. To realize the meaning of the verbal messages wider and to analyze people's behavior, we have to understand both the primary meaning of the nonverbal messages and their primary functions. The functions of the nonverbal messages are the following:

1. **Contradicting** (negation of verbal messages) – your face is writhed, you have necked eyes, your eyebrows are frowning. You are screaming with a red, angry look: „I'm not angry!", sending at the same moment a double message – the nonverbal cues represent one thing while the words – another.

2. **Regulating** (control person-to-person interaction) – the non-verbal cues establish the „turn-taking", said differently „the rules of order" during a conversation. The gestures, eye contact and voice tone usually assist in control the alternate who continues to speak that directs the flow of verbal exchanges. The regulatory skills of others affect our mind. For example, after explaining your opinion on an issue, you raise and then deepen intonation and say, "… that's why I feel the way I do." The intonation in compliance with silence signals you are finished speaking

and another person may start to discuss. So, your behavior impacts the flow of verbal interaction.

3. **Emphasizing** – this function of the nonverbal cues allows stressing or laying an emphasis on a verbal message. For example, somebody waves the finger censoriously, raising and depressing the voice (just to demonstrate the anger), with an intention to stress series of words and says: „It's your fault, not mine!" The nonverbal cues are used to emphasize the behavior.

4. **Substituting** – the nonverbal cues can substitute (replace) the spoken words or speech. There are some cases when we don't know what to say, how to express our sorrow, pain or disappointment. A shrug of the shoulders is commonly used instead of "I don't know"; the up-and-down nod is understood as „yes"; a forming of the letter „T" with your hands during some sports events is understood as "time-out".

5. **Complementing** – it means „reinforcing" of a verbal message. The head of the employee is bowed and the body is hunched as the boss tells him/her how vain is his/her job performance. The nonverbal cues provide the clues to the relationship an employee and the boss share.

To improve the ability to analyze another person and to „read" him/her better, we use the following nonverbal messages (clues):

• **Kinesics** – this clue includes a variety of facial expressions we usually call it mime, body posture, gestures, eye movement, walking speed. Appraisal information is contained in the look on your face, whether you look aside or stare, whether your shoulders are slouched or straight, whether your gait suggests a zeal or worries or whether your lips signal disregard with a smirk or are curved in a smile. The prime communicator of emotions is our face, you can't hide them in any case. It affects whether other persons evaluate you to be submissive or dominant (do you remember, we usually say, "a face as cold as ice", "a baby face", "a face as strong as a bulldog's" etc.). The eyes are also a crucial component of interpersonal communication, the messages you send with eyes may be valued in a variety of ways, the central functions of eye movements are the following: revealing of the extent of interest to our conversation partner (the pupils of the eyes react to information); regulation of person-to-person interaction; affecting the opinions (mind) and perception of obedience or dominance. The distinctive posture of a person (remember, we can detect a person on his/her shadow) can distinguish him/her from others and allows identifying them easily. The unconscious movements of the body, the so-called „emblems" are sent consciously and translated easily into speech (wave with a finger that is understood like "come here", a thumbs-up gesture that means "okay"); „illustrators" are used deliberately to facilitate the tasks (when you give directions to someone); „regulators" – these are the cues that are used intentionally to affect alternating participation (gazing at somebody talking encourages a person to continue speaking).

• **Paralinguistics** – these are some messages commonly sent by means of our voice. It means not the content of people's speech, but the way how information is provided. The vocal cues assist to define the true meaning of the person's speech (to read between the lines), it is of great value at the minute when we are considering whether someone is sarcastic in relation to our words or not (Example: the words "Yeah, right" express various meanings depending on whether they are spoken sarcastically or sincerely. The interpretation of the spoken words affects how we respond to the person who told them). The essential components of this clue are - volume (the voice power influences perception of intended meaning), pitch (the lowness or highness of people's voices; the high-pitched voices are frequently associated with tension, feebleness, nervousness and are inherent to women; the low-pitched voices are associated with sexiness, strength, maturity), rate (the vocal cue that affects the communication of meaning. A rate has an influence on others' judgments of our mood and intensity), the word's pronunciation and articulation of a person (it is a way somebody pronounces the sounds. The focus of pronunciation is the way a person says the words correctly; mispronouncing the words may sustain a loss of confidence), silence and hesitations (a basic knowledge here is knowing when making a pause and wait for reaction. Slowing the rate of speech, brief periods of silence and pauses allows gathering our thoughts).

• **Proxemics** (space and distance talks) – distance and physical proximity give a warning of disinterest in communicating or conversely a desire to be in contact with others. The closer people stand, the more they like one another, it indicates also how humble or dominant the persons are in a relationship. The next types of distances differentiate the kinds of interactions and the relationships that we share: intimate distance (ranges from skin contact to 18 inches from conversation partner. People usually share closeness with those to whom they trust and with whom they could share an emotional bond); personal distance (ranges from 18 inches to 4-5 feet; we mostly converse informally. This distance is used commonly at social events or when talking during coffee breaks or between classes), social distance (from 4-5 feet to 12 feet. At this distance, we are less friendly talking about personal business and more able to keep our conversation partner at arm's length. Such conversations happen during meetings, conferences, meals and are held within a social distance range), public distance (from 12 feet and more. It is the distance we exploit to keep away physically from interaction or to communicate with strangers. Public distances are much less likely than smaller distances to envisage interpersonal communication).

• **Haptics** (touch) - is generally drawn into the close relationships between the persons, it indicates the desire for closeness. Touch seems to be an important tool in interpersonal communication that applied for various purposes of the conversation partners: to encourage affiliation, to predominate, to show our concern for others. Touch is an effective way of demonstrating both support or effect, it is of great importance for the maintenance of our psychological or physiological health, as people get older they are often touched less. An individual who initiates touch is also the one who commonly regulates, directs or controls the interaction, he/she is frequently more assertive that someone, who is touched. Touch gives signals of dominance, dislike, outrage or aggression; the amount of the consensual touching indicates how people like each other.

• **Appearance and artifactual communication** – the reactions are under the influence of both appearance and artifactual communication. During the first stage of a relationship, our looks and clothes affect the first impressions that may lead to our being rejected or accepted. Jewelry and clothing can cause surrounding persons to form judgments regarding our character, success, competence and power. People usually respond more positively to those who are well and neatly dressed than those whose outfit is questionable or unacceptable. Numerous researchers of the recent years have discovered that our clothes affects our cognitive processes. It appears frequently that slimmer people, tall men and lusty women are awarded a premium for their beauty, height and thinness. For example, while speaking about height, taller people seem to win jobs and elections; when it comes to weight, individuals who are overweight or corpulent are treated more unkindly, they usually earn less than slim or people of average weight.

• **Olfactics** (smell) - smell is intimately linked to recall of good and bad memories. If something negative or bad occurs, for example, our odor sense sharpens, warning us of impending danger. We have good recalls associated with the presence of pleasant smells, such as flowers blooming, freshly baked cookies. People usually mask their natural smells with perfumes, deodorants, aromatherapy oils just to induce positive emotions like romance, friendship or sexual arousal.

• **Color** (associations and connections) – the colors we wear affect us both emotionally and physically. Color may help force us to move more slowly or quickly, help us relax. For example, people who prefer to wear regularly red color tend to be more outgoing, active, impatient than those who avoid this color.

• **Chronemics** (the communicative value of time) – it is the study of how people use time to communicate. Some persons are preoccupied with time, while others waste it on a regular basis. Miscalculations, disagreements and misunderstandings involving time can create a relationship and communication problems. Some of us are typically early, while others are chronically late, somebody prefers a more leisurely pace while others approach life with a sense of urgency. We plan our time with an aim to ensure we achieve all needed tasks. How long one is willing to wait for somebody (for something) is also a kind of reflection of our state and the sense we place on what we are waiting for.

These ultimate nonverbal clues assist us in understanding and analyzing people better, especially our conversation partners.

Chapter Two: Using verbal communication to analyze people

Have you heard that the words a person says can tell us a lot about his/her personality? Do you know that a single word combination allows us to know a lot about his/her real needs? Analyzing people's words enables you to know about the things people are usually trying to hide. Our success depends upon our ability to communicate with people efficiently, both by nonverbal means and verbally. These types of communications affect our interactions with others in private relationships and in business, as well as physical and psychological well-being and our personal and financial success.

The certain word combinations reflect routinely the characteristics of a person's behavior who speaks them. The so-called „word clues" amend the credibility of „reading" the behavioral characteristics of the individuals by exploring the word combinations and cliches they choose during speaking. The word combination alone can't appoint an individual's personal attributes, but still, they supply valuable information on an individual's thought process as well as characteristics of behavior. The brain of human beings is utterly capable. We use mostly verbs and nouns, whilst the adverbs, adjectives, and other parts of the speech are almost added at the subconscious level during the conversation of the thoughts into speech. These words we supplement allow combing through what we are thinking in reality and what archetype we actually are. A person, for example, repeats a certain word several times: "This voice is very strong", "I don't have the strength to continue studying", "A man whose car is really powerful". At first sight, these expressions may seem like quite unrelated statements, but on the other point of view, the word "power" or rather its synonyms were mentioned in each sentence.

The allocation of the vocabulary inside the mind doesn't happen in a random order, but the said words and phrases are usually confined to our core needs, desires, and concerns. Otherwise speaking, a man who said the above-mentioned phrases, is deeply concerned about strength, power and, of course, weakness. He, probably, wants to be strong or he might be concerned about becoming more powerful or he might be thinking that he needs to be stronger.

The other example shows us what we conclude from the stories people tell us: "Two days ago I was walking with a couple of my friends and a huge stranger came out of the blue. My friends and I thought that he was holding a course for our company to show hackles or something like this, but at the last moment he looked away and went by". So what could we conclude from this story? Do you remember the first story about a man who was thinking about power and strength? This story was also told by the same person, who was concerned about strength and power. The phrase "huge stranger" shows that person's primary goal was to be or to seem strong both, physically or emotionally. Of course, you might consider that any person would have told the narrative in the same manner, but the thing that the man left out all the unnecessary details and focused only on the stranger's size show, that this is the only thing he was interested in. From this example we can easily analyze a man telling us this story, that he is really anxious about power and strength, he may even feel himself as a not enough strong or powerful. How do you think, does memory work randomly? No, it's not true, we just remember the things that have affected us mostly. Just think, you are very likely to memorize an event that has come out stronger than such one that didn't really affect you. If this story was told by different people, some details and trifles would certainly be prevalent, but new ones would appear exactly and some of the old ones would be left out. The other important thing about our person we can analyze from this story is that this man has a problem with worrying. Everything that happened was just a result of his sense or perception («…but at the last moment he looked away and went by…») but is not a result of a real-life event. The stranger just came out of the blue and didn't do something to them, maybe he didn't even want to hurt somebody, but because of a man's worries, he thought, that the stranger wanted to harm them.

The basic sentences that form the verbal communication consist mostly of a subject and, of course, a verb. Let's consider the sentence "He walked." So, it is combined with the pronoun "He" and the verb "walk" in past tense. Other words added to this construction depict both the quality of the noun „He", tense and action of the verb. Such advised changes provide special clues to a person's characteristics of behavior. These clues help us to disclose an assumption or to suppose about the behavioral characteristics. Just an example, the above-mentioned structure "He walked and the word „quickly" makes "He walked quickly." The verbal clue "quickly" assigns a meaning of haste, but this clue doesn't denote the reason for such haste. The walk might be quicker if somebody (a man) is behind for an essential meeting or intends he could miss this one. The conscientious persons consider themselves always as trusted and responsible and do not want in any way to be late for important meetings and events. Persons who wish to be on time always honor generally accepted social norms, they want to justify the expectations of possible surrounding persons. The persons with such behavior are good employees because they do everything to avoid the disappointment of their employers.

The word clue presented by the verbal communication provides a noninvasive mean to analyze people effectively without familiarity. The following examples will demonstrate how the word clue provides valuable information on the behavioral characteristics of people during their speech.

• „She won another prize" - The word clue "another" describes a thought, that the speaker has already won more than one prize. The person wanted to stress that others know exactly she/he won at least one other prize, promoting in such a manner her self-image and prestige. The winner may be amenable to the flattery of others despite the envious persons, just to strengthen her self-affirmation. The spectators could exploit this soft spot by using ego-enhancing comments and flattery.

• „A boy worked actively to attain his aim" - The word clue "actively" supposes the boy values aims that are complicated to attain for him. The aim, the boy has attained, is more complicated and difficult than the previous aims. The word clue "actively" also suspects that the boy can postpone enjoyment or meaning that active work and selflessness could produce better results. A job seeker with such characteristic would doubtless make a good employee, tenacity, and patience as eligibilities of his character.

• „A student sat through lectures with restraint" - The word combination " with restraint " represents some assumptions. The lecture was rather boring. Probably he had other fish to fry that's why he was impatient. Nevertheless, he was engaged with something other than the rather boring content of the lecture, he waited with restraint for a break before he left the class. It is maybe a student who follows etiquette and, of course, social norms. For example, an individual who receives a phone call can immediately get up and leave the classes or lectures even without asking permission. So it is a human being who probably does not follow generally accepted norms. Persons with strict social norms are better employees, as they maintain the rules and respect authority. Alternatively, a person who doesn't maintain the rules would doubtless be suited for a job that requires unequaled thinking. A person with the prepossession to act outside social rules would be a better spy than that one who is disposed to maintain social conventions because the spies are frequently asked to violate social norms.

• „She concluded to purchase that jacket" - The verb "concluded" reflects that a woman or a girl evaluated diverse options before to make a right solution for the purchasing a jacket. Probably she made efforts to some degree prior to rendering a decision to buy. This behavior trait supposes the woman thinks things through, particularly if the gain was a minor one. The usual verb "concluded" reflects that the speaker is a woman of impulse, who could likely say: "I just bought that jacket."

The adverb "just" means that this customer bought the thing without giving the decision much thought. The verbal clue "concluded" helps us to develop a belief that the speaker (a woman) is an introvert, who commonly thinks before performing some acts. These individuals carefully weight all the pros and cons before making a decision. The persons who are extroverts are frequently more impulsive, even hot-blooded. The use of the verb "concluded" does not positively determine this person as an introvert, but it does provide an indication that she might be an introvert. An exact personality assessment needs a more comprehensive psychological assessment; nevertheless, a spectator can exploit a person if she knows that person tends toward introversion or extroversion. The human beings who are extroverts fuelled by the other individuals and seek arousal from their environments. They often speak effortlessly without thinking for a long time and use with full confidence the trial-and-error method; whereas the introverts waste their own energy when they participate socially and try to recharge themselves their „batteries". These individuals seek a motivation that's why they mostly keep a silent, weighing all the details before making clear, weighted solutions. Before entering into the business negotiations, knowing whether your adversary tends toward introversion or extroversion can provide a strategic and important superiority. The sellers should provide the introverted customers with enough time to make a decision accordingly all the sales proposals. Such customers acquire information, think it over and only then make a solution. Putting pressure on this kind of people with a goal to make impulsive or quicker solutions may respond them with a definite no because it is out of their rules to make immediate solutions. The extroverts, conversely, might be pressured to some medium degree to make urgent decisions because they are susceptible to it. Many people reveal both characteristics. Furthermore, those who are introvert and who are comfortable on the skin, often show behaviors that could be associated with extroverts. Could you imagine that a person may be analyzed through such a little sentence, consisting of six words?

• „He has done a proper solution" - The verbal clue "proper" suggests that the speaker wrestled with himself, with a moral, ethical or legal dilemma and surpassed some level of external or internal opposition to render a proper solution. This feature of the behavior reflects that this individual has appropriate strength and emphasis of the character to make the right conclusion even when repelled with opposing views.

These are common examples to show how a person's character and behavior by could be analyzed by just paying attention to the words. Using the verbal communication to "read" people better means not just an analysis of a single phrase, but at least a sentence to get the correct results. You may also collect as many phrases as you can and put them jointly to find out what's common between them all. Analyzing people is easy. Listen attentively to what they say.

Chapter Three: 15 Gold Tips and Tricks for Reading People

One shouldn't be Sherlock Holmes to guess what's going on in somebody's head. Most of us don't realize essential signals that are always in our head, we just have to think through what certain gestures mean in order to address the issue. Unfortunately, there is no simple faultless way to guess what somebody is thinking, even the greatest intellectuals as well as wizards in the world are right only in 75-80% of the time. Logic won't tell us the true story about an individual. People may learn to analyze deeper both nonverbal and verbal cues that people share. The clue is to be objective and represent the received information impartially without straining the sense. Whether you're analyzing a chef, colleague or somebody else to understand them correctly, you must surrender jaundices. People who analyze the other individuals well are trained to „read" invisible meaning, i.e. to read between the lines. Some tricks and techniques of analyzing people are provided here, just remember, they all need to surrender pure logic in favor of receiving alternative forms of input.

1 Trick – **Preparing a basis**

Like at the beginning of any business, you should prepare here a so-called „baseline", to understand the main goal, methods, techniques, knowledge. To be able to analyze somebody, firstly, you should know this person as well as possible. By trying to know an individual personally, knowledge of the precedence, common habits as well as preferences may help in producing a good impress on a conversation partner. Just imagine, you have a friend who is very fussy. Taking into account this characteristic, such fuss doesn't mean obligatory irritability or a pack of lies. Imagine, you met him/her out of doors, basic skills would consider him/her as nervous or worried. Instead, he/she has an inflamed hand that pains him.

2 Trick – **Take notice of appearance**

While analyzing an individual pay attention: Is he/she putting on a business costume with highly polished boots, dressed for happiness and success? Do a sports jersey or a sweatshirt and trousers indicate ride comfort combining being casual? Look at people's faces. Keep in sight the impermanent look. Examine people as close as it is possible to see if there are any almost imperceptible movements of their mouth that disclose what people are indeed thinking about. Imagine, somebody may smile at you, but if his/her lips twitch, it might signal that he/she is thinking of something unbearable. Anything squeezed or stretched even for a little time, maybe a sign. Our furrowed brows or a tense jaw signals a worry.

3 Trick - **Notice posture**

While analyzing person's posture, one may put the following questions: Does the individual, that are analyzed, hold his/her head high? Does an individual walk indecisively or hunch? Standing up straight on the shoulders back means a power position; it means to maximize the amount of space you just fill. Hunching or slouching is a result of destructing your form; it seems to take up less free space and to project less power. Keeping a right posture appoints respect, promotes engagement, regardless you are a leader in your team or not.

4 Trick - **Search body language**

The latest studies of the body language have determined the interesting fact – the words of human beings account only for five to six percent of the communication sense. The voice tone accounts for about 30-40% and the body language for 50-55%! So, it means the body language provides us with the great amount of valuable information. This includes thoughts of the human beings, but, of course, if you already know how and when to pay your attention. Body language tells a lot, especially, if the communicating persons are well disposed towards each other. It could be an interpersonal issue or wondering off the topic at hand. Here you find some general clues that depict comfortable/ uncomfortable level.

Comfortable signs are: smile must be not gritted and forced; eye contact; flaccid limbs. On the contrary, not comfortable body language signs: fold legs and hands (it expects avoidance behavior, self-defense or even wrath). While crossing the legs someone tries to point the toes of the top leg towards the individual he/she is most commonly with); looking away while talking, absence of the eye contact; limbs are moving all the time -- a lot of nervous tapping of the leg or fingers (when someone bites or licks his/her lips they are trying to calm themselves in an disagreeable situation); pushing aside from the speaker (people lean commonly away from the individuals they do not like and, on the contrary, toward those they like); pushing aside hands (somebody places his/her hands in the pockets, put them behind their back it means that they are keeping back something).

5 Trick - **Interpret expressions of the face**

The emotions can be engraved on people's faces. A brow furrow means over-thinking or even a worry. The crumpled lips mean contempt, anger, malice, spite. The cracking teeth or a clenched jaw signal of tension. While talking, watch humans as close as possible, a faint smile gives away what individuals are really feeling. If the eyes of your conversation partner close for longer than usual, perhaps they're stumbling and taking a second trying to grasp the meaning of a situation. Generally, it is a guide of someone who is running out of control.

6 Trick - **Notice challenges in the baseline**

A normally tenacious individual who seems not to be physically present and doesn't wish to get near someone with a 10-12-foot pole has something going on. Once you have observed the way an individual acts in daily living, keep a watch for a while for the stuff that doesn't mesh. If something doesn't occur, you have to ask about the reason. The conversation partners could be exhausted, have showdown with others, have some small personal issue that's sticking in their craw or got yelled by the chef. It mustn't be considered as a reflection of your relationships with that individual before you have all the details and trifles.

7 Trick - **Watch the eyes of the speaker**

The eyes can transmit powerful energy. The brain has an electromagnetic signal falling beyond the scope of the body. The numerous researchers specify that the eyes produce the same signal too. Take a minute to inspect the eyes. Are they seems to be calm, angry, crafty? The children probably grew up hearing frequently: "You! Look me in the eye, while you are talking to me!" The elder persons operated usually with the help of the theory, it could be perilous to hold an individual's gaze while you're lying, and they were right. Everybody knows, people don't want to retain the eye contact when they wish to conceal some information and mostly the case they are lying. The bigger part of such liars compensates with usury a pack of lies. While chatting with someone who is gazing and squirming, particularly if he/she is unblinking and still—he is lying to you.

8 Trick - **See if your conversation partners touch you**

People usually share the emotional power by way of physical contact like a flow of electricity. By analyzing surrounding persons, ask yourself, if it is warm, comfortable or pleasant for you during a hug or a handclasp of somebody? Is it so unpleasant, that you would better withdraw this? People's hands could be clammy, signaling troubles and anxiety. If an individual frequently embraces you when he/she sees you, but now he/she don't do this, it might mean that he/she feels intention towards you. Likewise, think about a weak handshake, it could mean uncertainty or nervousness. There such persons among our familiars that we don't want to touch them and want to be touched by them. Why? We don't want to be intimate with them, it's easy. Touching is private. Everybody has various notions of a "personal bubble", somebody who may touch you a lot doesn't definitely mean you are "in". If you are inquisitive according someone's touching habits toward you, just observe them around other people to understand where the norm is.

9 Trick - **Observe how far away the people are spatially**

The distance individual is close or far from you provides some penetration into his/her state of mind. If someone is distancing from you physically, it may mean that he/she does not want to be intimately or familiar (see the previous trick); it could also mean they're in a hurry and don't want to be late for some important event, everything depends on a situation. Some of us are not comfortable being within a stated or physical proximity of others irrespective the case. Keeping a distance by somebody is not obligatory a reflection of you. The same goes for the other side of the spectrum – some people have no concept of private space: if they violate your private space, they could not even think about it. That doesn't mean any important sense for them.

10 Trick - **Listen to the voice tone**

Have you ever thought about the interesting fact, how blind people can distinguish persons? How can they understand where the mom or dad is, a stranger or a thief? How do they realize the mood and the intentions of others? Try to tell lies them and you'll understand the sense.

The individual's tone and volume of the voice tell us a lot about emotions and thoughts insight us. The sound frequencies create the vibrations. When you are analyzing people, make clear to how their voice tone impresses on you. Does their tone sound quiet? Or is it gruff? A person's voice tells us a lot about feelings. Listen attentively for challenges or pitch of the individual's voice you would like to analyze. Pay attention to volume: are they talking quieter or louder than usual? Notice, if they are hedging using their voice, saying "Oh..." commonly. This may mean, they are a little nervous. Pay an attention, if the tone expresses an emotion that they are not expressing plainly. Do they sound angry or maybe sarcastic? They may have a sensation the necessity to passively regain control.

11 Trick – **Notice the word choice**

When the persons say the phrases or sentences, there is usually a cause underlying the content (Remember Chapter two, where we have considered an example of the word order in a sentence). If somebody tells you: "You're dating another dentist?" The usage of the word "another" means that they are saying in fact: "You just dated a dentist and he went to crap, so now you are going to date another one?" The constructions "no/yeah" are quite popular today. These small two-letter words could be an irrefutable piece of evidence for ambiguity (or for distinctness).

12 Trick – **Ask questions**

Imagine, you should „read" a person. It means you are listening, watching and observing your conversation partner. Don't forget to ask questions and make a pause.

Just sit back, wait and take notice. Remember, that you should ask the short questions. The long questions are difficult to understand and moreover to get that answer, you wanted to get. If you ask: "How is your dad?" You, probably, get an incoherent, dissipated response that wouldn't help you to evaluate the information you are actually looking for. The speaker may answer: „Good, thanks", and nothing more. It is a deadlock. What are you going to do then? But if you ask: "What book are you reading now?", you may be able to acquire more private information. The vague, open-ended questions do not work as usual because if the person shoots the breeze, it becomes more difficult to detect any falseness. Ask the questions that require a straight answer and don't be a meddler! After asking a question, observe without interrupting.

13 Trick – **Feel emotional energy**

Emotions of the persons are an impressive expression of the energy. We point these with intuition. Some people feel good to be around; they improve your vitality and mood. The others are tiresome that you instinctively want to buzz off. This "slender energy" can be feet from the body, though it is invisible.

14 Trick - **Listen to intuition**

The intuition is not what your brain says, just what your gut feels. It is a kind of nonverbal information, you recognize via images, body knowing, not via logic. Trying to analyze somebody, think over who is this person, not his/her attire. Intuition allows an individual to see further than the evident to disclose a richer story. We always rely upon our intuition. If we don't know the course of business or if we don't know how to act in some situations, we say „we trust our intuition" and it helps.

An ultimate list of subconscious means is following: 1. Keep gut feelings – Tune in to what the inward nature says, during first meeting or conversation with partners, an inner reaction takes place prior you get a chance to speak. Inward nature appears rapidly, being the first response; they are the inside truth gauge of you, ensuring you if you can charge people or not; 2. Draw attention the outbreaks of insight - various chatting may provide you with "Ah-ha" effect. Be on the lookout, in another case, you might let it through; 3. The goosebumps are intuitive shiver that expresses that we resonate with people who put some fight into us or are saying something that cut to the quick. They may also appear when you endure a dejavu, a clarification that you have known somebody (something) before, though you have in fact never met; 4. Be attentive for instinctive empathy - sometimes we may feel person's emotions and physical symptoms in our own body, that is an intense form of empathy.

15 Trick - **Detect a liar**

Among various reasons why we learn the individual's analyzing and all the possible techniques related to the case, is to analyze and to detect a person as a liar. A huge variety of techniques are already presented in the book, the methods of nonverbal and verbal communication, allow us to analyze deeper a person that is interesting to us. When searching somebody to see if he/she is lying, you should look for a language of our body and the cues that incline to nervousness. Notice carefully if somebody's voice or a body language changes once and again. It is rather easy if a wife/husband usually touches and embraces you all the time, but suddenly stops to do this with no reasons, he/she may lie you when you are asking them for the reason. But, do not hurry up, a person who doesn't make eye contact or who keeps his/her head on a swivel, should not be a liar, there is no relation sometimes between lying and making an eye contact.

Still, people tell a lie even without thinking a little that it could be detected easily by an expert or even by a beginner who knows all the tricks. Some of us are inveterate liars, so it could be hardly found where the lie is.

And one more comment: work in clusters. Noticing one cue is not a base for making a conclusion. Somebody could be leaning away from you, just because that chair is hard to get comfortable in. Try to take a cue from people's words, their body, tone, their face. Once you get one from each and they are interrelated with each other, it may be safe to proceed. But through it, make sure you have three or four signs (tricks) before you start making conclusions. Being apprehensive about the people's feelings and their thoughts is an important skill in a life that will help everyone to navigate the interpersonal relationships.

Chapter Four: Decoding personality types

Have you ever wished you knew a technique to decode an individual's peculiarity type at first view? The life, habits, relations, friends, and family or career makes us searching solutions to interpret people's behavior and comprehend them. Would it be a little dull? There are no fixed physical features that concern for a pointed personality type, but still, there are opportunities that you can suspect an individual's preference basing on his/her conduct. Here are some types of behaviors that will provide you with the clues to somebody's preferences:

1. *How quickly does the person respond to a question?* (Introvert or extrovert)

I hope, you haven't forgotten chapter two „using verbal communication to analyze people", where we have examined an example of an individual type like extrovert and introvert? When you put the question, pay attention, if an individual starts chatting rapidly without reflecting for a long time that seems like he/she almost thinking aloud? Do they take a minute or more to make a response and then they give considered and comprehensive response? Those who are introverts need to have a good look at making a response, while people who are extroverts truly need to think aloud in most cases. An introvert usually likes obtaining his/her power from considering the notions, thoughts, memories, responses that are inside their heads. They like doing something alone or with a particular amount of persons they feel comfortable with. The introverts usually take a moment to consider that they have a thought of what would be their further actions the ideas are in turn the defendant things for them. The next affirmations could mainly apply to them: they are seen as "discreet" or "despondent"; sometimes they waste time thinking all the actions through and do not dare to move into action at once; to be alone and to do the things alone is for them more comfortable than doing something in cooperation with somebody; that's why they would rather know well just a few people; individuals, who are introverts, frequently neglect to check with the outer space if their ideas really get the experience.

What about extroverts? They like obtaining the power from dynamic engagement in events and having a lot of various pursuits. They are excited to be in public settings and like to move other people to action. The extroverts often realize a challenge better when they speak aloud about this business. The following affirmations could basically apply to the extroverts: They feel comfortable in larger troops and like cooperating with them; they are acquainted with lots of people and have a wide circle of friends; they may change too quickly a kind of activity and don't need a long time to mull over; sometimes they start a project and neglect to stop and get precise on what they want to do and why.

You may make certain if this decoding of personality type works, conducting such an experiment: For example, you are an extrovert speaking with an introvert. Put any question, stop chatting and count to ten.

2. *Do they reflect on what is taking place now or has taken place already, or do they reflect about what is going to take place in the nearest future?* (Intuition and sensing)

Persons who like sensing are passed over what takes place now, at this moment. This person may always remind the others to live in the present instead of thinking about what might happen or what has happened already. People, who prefer sensing pay attention to physical reality, what they hear, taste, touch, and smell; they hold an interest in the present, actual, current and real. They frequently notice facts and remember details seems to be important.

Those who trust intuition are often blamed for looking at the world through rose colored glasses. Taking notice to the sense and kind of the information, they are inquired about new things, so they ponder more about the future than the past. This category of people would rather work more with abstract doctrines. The following characteristics may be a clue cheat sheet by decoding a personality type who is almost relayed on intuition: remembering the events "between the lines"; solving challenges by leaping between various opportunities and ideas; they would rather see the whole picture, then to examine trivial matters; they trust symbols, sensations, metaphors more than what they actually experience.

3. *How mindful are the people of how others will be driven by a solution?* (Thinking and feeling)

This predilection depicts a way the individuals like to make solutions. Do they like to put more weight than others on impersonal facts and principles (thinking) or do they put more weight on personal concerns (feeling)? But don't muddle feelings with emotions. Everybody has emotions concerning the decisions they resolve. The same fact is about the confusion of intelligence with thinking. Those who prefer feeling run everything through such a position of "How will this affect surrounding persons?" before taking any action. They trust it is possible to make the best solutions by weighting what people take care of; they are concerned with a thought, what is the best for the people that are in. They prefer to do whatever will observe or establish harmony.

The next affirmations generally apply to the individuals, who prefer feeling: strict commitment to others and their view; commitment with harmony and disappointment when it is missing; resolving with heart and a strong wish to be merciful; being tactful is more essential than telling the "bare" truth.

Those who prefer thinking are objective by nature and believe everybody else should be too. When these people make a decision, they like to find the basic truth, regardless of a situation involved. They like to analyze all pros and cons, and then be consistent in deciding; they try to be impersonal. This doesn't mean that thinkers do not attend to others, but common sense is a feature they learn while growing and developing. Among the preferences of those who prefer thinking are: enjoying scientific and technical fields where logic is of great importance; noticing inconsistencies; holding an opinion that telling the truth is more essential than being tactful; looking for logical explanations or solutions; these people could be seen as too task-oriented or indifferent.

4. *Does an alteration in arrangements rock their world or enhance it?* (Judging and perceiving)

The fourth predilection pair of decoding types depicts the way the individuals like to live their external life, what are the behaviors others tend to see? Do they prefer a more flexible and adaptable lifestyle (perceiving) or a more decided and structured lifestyle (judging)?

Every person is extrovert occasionally. This pair describes whether a person is extrovert when he/she is resolving solutions or when he/she is accepting essential information. Some of us deal with the outside when they acquire information. Other individuals do their interacting when they are rendering a decision. It doesn't signify whether they are using a perceptional predilection or a thinking predilection; they are still dealing with the external world. When it comes to dealing with the outward, the persons who look toward to focus on rendering solutions give their preference for judging based on the reason they are prone to prefer things determined. Those who are apt to concentrate on accepting information prefer perceiving by reason of staying open to a bottom line in order to get more information. Don't muddle judging and perceiving with a level of organization of somebody. Either, preference can be formed.

Now, take a moment to put a question to yourself which of the next definitions seem more opportune, easy-to-use for you? Those who like a more adjusted lifestyle seem to others as they choose an unprompted and spontaneous way of life. They like to realize the world more than organize it. They are open for acceptance of new information and knowledge. Remember, in type, the word „perceiving" means "preferring to take in information", that does not signify to be "perceptive" in terms of having quickly and exact perceptions about the events and people. The following affirmations generally apply to those, who prefer a more adaptable lifestyle: they are open to responding to whatever occurs; they usually work in bursts of energy and being stimulated by the forthcoming deadline; they like rather layout to a minimum.

As for those, who prefer a structured life pattern, they seem to prefer a well-planned or regiment style of living, they prefer ordered and settled, like to control everything as much as possible and feel confident when decisions are thought-out and made. Do not muddle judging with judgmental, in its negative direction about the occurrences and individuals; they are not related. The next affirmations are mainly applied to those persons who prefer structured lifestyle: they seem to be assignment oriented; they always compound long lists of proceedings to do and prefer to have all the proceedings decided; they follow the proverb „work hard, play hard" that's why they plan work just to shun rushing before a deadline. On the issue, they sometimes focus so much on the goal and may miss new information.

Having discussed the general types of decoding personalities, you may check your gain knowledge, decoding the personality types of the following example: It was late afternoon and everybody was hungry. Jack said to his friend Jim, he wanted to have dinner tonight, he liked seafood. He suggested to go to the "Joe's Crab Shack" or to the "Red Lobster". Jim agreed and chose the "Red Lobster". After some minutes passed, and all were ready to go to the restaurant, Jack suddenly said, they could also eat tacos tonight. His old friend had told him earlier about the great place near his house. It seemed strange Jack was the first one who had suggested Jim the first two restaurants. Jim said, he thought the decision was already made and they had chosen the "Red Lobster". Jack rebuffed and said resentfully, he had just suggested another place and Jim didn't need to get huffy about it. How can you decode these personality types?

Chapter Five: Communication styles of different personalities

The personality preferences influence their communication styles, that is also based on nature and innate factors. All the communication styles have absolutely no wrong or right ones, they are different and provide diverse strengths and challenges that depends on the context. The persons with the same preferences derive pleasure from communication with each other due to the similarity. The golden rule of our life states: Treat others the same way you would like to be treated. Not everybody in the world communicates and responds to their environment in the same way. Some of us are very uncomfortable with public displays of praise situations while others enjoy basking in the glow of the limelight.

There are following communication styles of the personalities:

Extroverts (E) — "Let's talk about the following…"

-        Tend to interrupt others due to their enthusiasm

-        Fluent, rapid speech

-        Louder volume

-        It happens frequently they think aloud

-        Express and improve ideas through dialogue with others

-        Prefer face-to-face conversation over cooler media

Challenge: Extroverts usually intimidate other persons (especially if they are introverts) by interruptions and rapid speech

Strength: Easily connect with surrounding persons and are enthusiastic

Tip: Do not expound a lack of facial feedback within discourse as a lack of engagement. The introverts in turn do not express the same level of external enthusiasm as the extroverts do.

Introverts (I) — "Let me get back to you…."

The general characteristics of communication style are the following:

-        Pause in responding or providing information

-        Quiet and calm voice volume

-        Speaking in shorter sentences, laconism

Challenge: Introverts often have problems with thinking quickly in response to unanticipated cases or questions

Strength: this category of people responds quietly and have a calming presence

Tip: Be sure you tell what is on your mind, do not expect the other persons to read your mind and be quicker than you. Ask the topics be tabled for discussion and comments after the meeting to allow for your best input.

If somebody prefers making solutions based upon present or past experiences, and he/she prefers to concrete both ideas and "facts" that could be observed, then this person lean towards sense. In other cases, if a person enjoys abstract ideas and likes imagining, especially the meaning behind the things you see and focusing on future possibilities, then he/she leans towards intuition. One of the persons prefers to run various tests carefully before beginning the new projects, the second one, conversely, doesn't mind experimenting with new efforts without all the proving at hand. These concepts reflect how different types of people perceive the world around through their subjective perceptions or their senses.

Sensors (S) — "Could you tell me details and facts, please"

The general characteristics of communication style are the following:

-       Ask for exact instructions and step-by-step information

-       Often use "what" and "how" questions

-       Are observant and attend to details

-       Use precise descriptions

Challenge: In respect of their need to know all the trifles and details on the topic, they may slow up possible discussions with contributions and questions

Strength: this category is able to relay a great number of facts and details about a discussed topic. They are very practical and realistic persons.

Tip: Keep up with the need for meaningful details may stop or slow down an information exchange or creative discussion.

Intuitive (N) — "Looking at the big picture…"

This communication style is characterized by following points:

-        Ask for the possible purpose of the actions

-        Looking for possibilities

-        Ask "why"-questions

-        Abstract terms, talking in general

Challenge: Have a tendency to talk abstractly about the topics and may neglect the details that make their contribution precise and clear; may appear to others to be obscure or off-topic.

Strength: Such people are able to see patterns in conversations and information while others do not pay attention to this

Tip: Acknowledge that other individuals need to test out or gain insight into your innovative ideas and thoughts. Keep up that your natural leaps may embarrass others — so specificate and detalize the leaps where it is possible for the audience. Provide content for the leaps and don't assume others understand.

Thinking (T) — "Let's be objective …"

This communication style is characterized by following points:

-        This type may communicate by testing you or your knowledge

-        Provide honest and apparent feedback

-        Are not over-enthusiastic by what others have decided

-        Are quick to analyze things and events, evaluate and critique

-        May appear crusty due to objectivity

Challenge: Will disregard if the talker appears to shoot the breeze

Strength: these persons are easy to follow depending on the logical structure of the communication

Tip: Recognize the value and importance of personal connection in discussion and the need for recognition and appreciation of those with a feeling preference. Learn to accept those at work who relish personal connection and endorsement — most likely they have a feeling preference.

Feeling (F) — "How will this affect/influence the other individuals?..."

Here we speak about:

-        Aspiration for harmony in the interaction

-        Talking about what they value

-        Enjoying cooperation and collaboration

-        Worrying about how others will be affected

-       Are quick to confirm meanings and show appreciation

Challenge: Will disregard when the others talk abstractly or when the impact on individuals is not being considered.

Strength: Incorporating with others and making it safe for them in conversations; try to be very diplomatic.

Tip: This type of people supports their arguments or views with logical reasoning and objective information. Focusing is based not only on the people involved but on the objectives and tasks. Accept that those with the thinking preference will compete, discuss and challenge other persons in conversation with a goal to get information and clarity.

Judging (J) — "Let's move on....."

Here we speak about following communication characteristics:

-       Impatient with too long descriptions, procedures

-       The tone seems to be like "hurry up — I want to make this decision"

-       May decide in advance

-       Enjoy decision making

-       Dislike interruptions or rambling

-       Tend to be precise

Challenge: Will disregard when other persons shoot the breeze or are slow to make a point. Their need for closure and structure may limit others and shut down information flow.

Strength: Like thinkers, the individuals with a judging preference use clearer structure. They are easy to follow in conversations and are mostly time-sensitive.

Tip: To escape cut off a discussion, try leaving discussions open that can be left open. Accept the value in "off-roading" versus always using the super highway in conversations. Avoid the clock, that is always ticking in your head reminding you of the passage of time.

Perceiving (P) — "Let's explore this more….."

Here we speak about following communication characteristics:

-        Seem to want "space" to make own solutions/decisions

-        Want more information to distinguish, more options to explore

-        Slow to decide or conclude

-        Like processing when speaking

Challenge: This type of conversational style may seem hard to follow by other individuals.

Strength: Involve a lot of information and digressive topics in their discussions that enhance the discussion. Information, the process, and research are more important than a conclusion.

Tip: Accept that your exploration style of conversation may seem like meandering to other persons and you may lose the listeners.

Conclusion

Why is it so essential understanding personalities? Just view the matter scientifically, it is a fun, but from a day-to-day life view, it means more than you could imagine. The better you comprehend other individuals, the more prosperous you will be in dealing with them in different life situations. Psychology is a scientific branch of learning, but understanding, moreover analyzing individual is a much more practical discipline. It is about applying psychology to your benefit and usefulness in everyday cases, to „read" people, to maintain, assist and impact, to get your point of view in a way that is essential for you, to understand better and make right decisions, to manage and justify people, and deal with disputable situations, and the most important - to operate and develop our own effect on the individuals.

From time to time it is essential to know more and differentiate between various types of people's characters. We know that training makes better, so using the temper testing can actually promote us, as it pulls down the entries into a notable case. Does somebody tend to refrain from intrinsically and reason out, or „speak aloud"? Do the persons prefer to be a pioneer or start dealing with the first occasion? Do they display a delicate diplomacy or a plain-dealing? Do the individuals like to get the case done before chilling, or do they chill then get the case done? We are all psychologists: we have families and friends, we go to the restaurants, we go to parties, we form a part of the big teams and we make our solutions about people all the time and every day; and often get it wrong. So let's start to get it right, it's so much more worth.

Author's Afterthoughts

תודה
Dankie Gracias
Спасибо شكراً Takk
Merci
Köszönjük Terima kasih
Grazie Dziękujemy Děkojame
Ďakujeme Vielen Dank Paldies
Kiitos Täname teid 谢谢
Thank You
Tak
感謝您 Obrigado Teşekkür Ederiz
감사합니다
Σας ευχαριστούμε ขอบคุณ
Bedankt Děkujeme vám
ありがとうございます
Tack

Thanks ever so much to each of my cherished readers for investing the time read this book!

I know you could have picked from many other books but you chose this one. So a big thanks for downloading this book and reading all way to the end.

If you enjoyed this book or received value from it, I'd like to ask you for a favor. Please take a few minutes to post an honest and heartfelt review on Amazon.com Your support does make a difference and to benefit other people.